C O N N E C T

MW01205593

Saying Goodbye

MARILYN S. ROSENTHAL
DANIEL B. FREEMAN

Series Editor: John Rosenthal

Boston   Burr Ridge, IL   Dubuque, IA   Madison, WI
New York   San Francisco   St. Louis
Bangkok   Bogotá   Caracas   Lisbon   London   Madrid   Mexico City
Milan   New Delhi   Seoul   Singapore   Sydney   Taipei   Toronto

McGraw-Hill

A Division of The **McGraw·Hill** Companies

Connections Readers: Saying Goodbye

This book is printed on acid-free paper.

domestic 1 2 3 4 5 6 7 8 9 0 DOC DOC 9 0 0 9 8 7
international 1 2 3 4 5 6 7 8 9 0 DOC DOC 9 0 0 9 8 7

ISBN 0-07-292779-8

Editorial director: Thalia Dorwick
Publisher: Tim Stookesberry
Development editor: Pam Tiberia
Production supervisor: Tanya Nigh
Print materials consultant: Marilyn Rosenthal
Project manager: Shannon McIntyre, Function Thru Form, Inc.
Design and Electronic Production: Function Thru Form, Inc.
Typeface: Goudy
Printer and Binder: R.R. Donnelley and Sons

Grateful acknowledgment is made for use of the following:
Still photography: Jeffrey Dunn, Ron Gordon, Judy Mason, Margaret Storm

Library of Congress Catalog Card Number: 97-75582

International Edition

http://www.mhhe.com

Rebecca Remembers

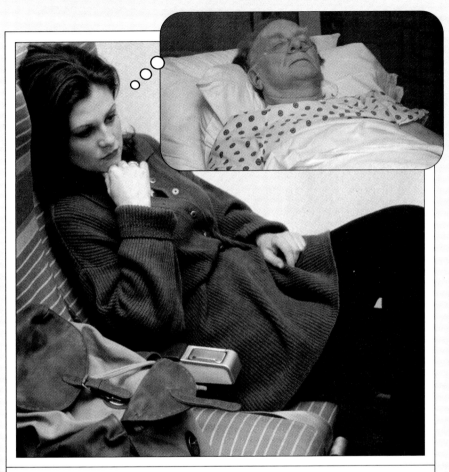

Rebecca Casey is on the plane. She's going home to Boston. She's worried about her father, Patrick. He's in the hospital. She's going to see him. She thinks about her father, and she thinks about her life in San Francisco.

Rebecca remembers the good times in San Francisco. She remembers the retirement party for Mr. and Mrs. Mendoza. Their sons, Alberto and Ramón, were there. Ramón's son, Alex, was there too.

Rebecca remembers her new home at Nancy Shaw's house. Her new friends welcomed her.

She remembers her friends at the San Francisco College of Music.

Rebecca remembers Emma Washington and the after-school program. She remembers Alex and his best friend, Vincent.

Rebecca remembers Alberto and the photo gallery.

Rebecca remembers long talks with Ramón. And then Rebecca thinks about her father again. She thinks about her family in Boston.

Rebecca thinks about her brother, Kevin. Kevin understood her dream about music school.

Rebecca thinks about her father. He wanted her in Boston—not San Francisco. But later he understood Rebecca's dream. He loves her, and she loves him. And now he's sick in the hospital. Her father and brother need her. Why did she leave Boston? What's going to happen now?

The Emergency

At the airport

1 How's Dad?

2 Not good. He's in the hospital.

Kevin is waiting for Rebecca at the airport. They meet and hug.

How did it happen?

Kevin tells Rebecca about their father.

"Dad had a heart attack. He fell."

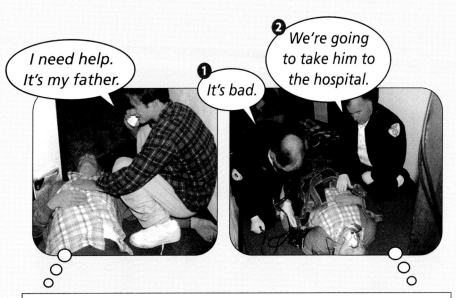

Kevin saw his father on the floor. He called for help. He called 911, the Emergency Medical Service (EMS). They came to the house. They helped Mr. Casey.

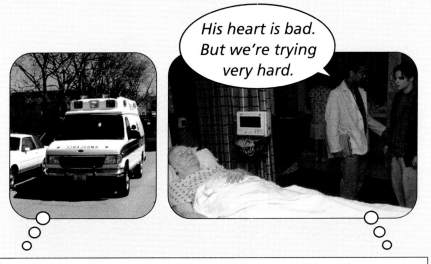

The EMS put Mr. Casey in an ambulance. They drove to the hospital. A doctor looked at Mr. Casey. He talked to Kevin about his father.

Kevin and Rebecca at the hospital

Rebecca talks to her father.

She shows him her mother's necklace.

Dr. Lincoln talks to Rebecca about her father.

At the Caseys' house

Rebecca and Kevin are very tired. They go home. Rebecca looks at the house. Things are all over the floor. The house is a mess. Rebecca is very sad. She sits alone and cries.

Rebecca is very angry at Kevin. They fight. Then the phone rings. It's the hospital.

7

Bad News

At the hospital

Kevin, I'm sorry. Let's not fight. I need you, and you need me right now.

Your father had another heart attack. It was very bad.

Kevin and Rebecca go back to the hospital. Rebecca feels bad. She is sorry about the fight with Kevin. Dr. Lincoln talks to Rebecca about her father.

1 Maybe you can call your father's brother.

2 But Dad never talked to Uncle Brendan.

3 Maybe they can talk now.

Rebecca and Kevin call a priest. Father O'Connor asks about their family. Rebecca remembers her father's brother, Brendan.

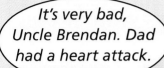

Rebecca calls Uncle Brendan. He lives on a farm in Illinois. Uncle Brendan is coming to the hospital.

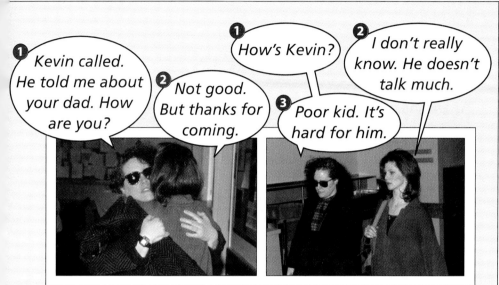

Sandy comes to the hospital. She asks about the Casey family.

Sandy and Rebecca have coffee together. Sandy asks Rebecca about California. Rebecca asks Sandy about Jack. Rebecca looks at Sandy's face. Sandy is crying. Jack hit Sandy.

Brothers

At the hospital

Brendan Casey comes to the hospital. He meets Kevin and Rebecca.

Brendan sees his brother, Patrick. They didn't talk for thirty years. They are both sorry. Patrick takes Brendan's hand.

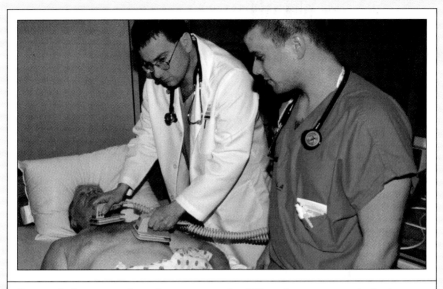

Patrick has another heart attack. The doctors can't help him. Patrick dies.

Brendan calls his wife, Anne, in Illinois. She's going to come to the funeral.

Rebecca calls Aunt Molly about the funeral. She also calls Patrick's friends.

They all come to Patrick's funeral.

At the funeral home

Brendan asks Kevin about the people there.

Rebecca and Anne talk about Patrick and Brendan.

Grief

At the funeral home

> **1** It's so sad. Kevin and Rebecca have no family now.

> **2** But they have us. Two aunts and an uncle. We're their family now.

Aunt Molly is talking to Brendan and Anne about Kevin and Rebecca.

> **1** We remember your father. He was a great fireman.

> **2** Thank you.

The fire chief of the Boston Fire Department gives Rebecca and Kevin a helmet. The helmet has a special meaning.

16

There are many people at the funeral. Frank Wells remembers Patrick.

Matt comes to the funeral.

Sandy comes, too.

At the cemetery

Patrick's family and friends go to the cemetery.

God, please take care of Patrick Casey.

Father O'Connor says a prayer for Patrick.

Kevin and Rebecca are very sad. They say goodbye to their father.

Life Goes On

At the Caseys' house

Brendan and Anne go back to the Caseys' house with
Rebecca and Kevin. They are all looking at the letters and
cards from family friends.

Kevin leaves the room. It's hard for Kevin. He's only 17. And now, he has no parents. Brendan and Anne are worried about him. They are also worried about Rebecca.

In the street

Kevin and Rebecca talk about their future. Kevin feels sad. He also feels angry and alone. He misses his father. He fights with Rebecca.

Kevin and Rebecca go home.

A Box of Memories

At the bank

> Yes, here it is. Patrick Casey and Rebecca Casey. You can look in the safe deposit box.

Kevin found a safe deposit box key in their father's room. It was from the Fleet Bank. Rebecca and Kevin are now at the bank.

Rebecca and Kevin look in the safe deposit box. They find letters, an Irish ring, a photo of Brendan and Patrick, and Patrick's insurance for $50,000.

Kevin and Rebecca leave the bank. Kevin is happy. He's thinking about the money.

Rebecca is worried. They need the money for college, rent, and many other things.

At the Caseys' house

1 Rebecca, I can live with my friends. I'm not a kid anymore. Please, go back to San Francisco.

2 I can't. It's too far away from you.

3 It's not so far. And there are phones. I can call you.

4 Let's not fight anymore. I'm going to think about it.

Rebecca and Kevin go back to the house. They talk about their future, and they fight again.

The Missing Car

At a restaurant

Rebecca and Kevin are at a restaurant with Brendan and Anne. They're eating oysters. Brendan likes them. Anne doesn't.

Rebecca tells them about the insurance money. She gives Brendan the Irish ring. It was Brendan's mother's ring. He gives it to Anne.

In the street

They leave the restaurant. Anne asks Rebecca about the future. Kevin gets angry again.

Kevin fights with Rebecca. He walks home alone.

Kevin goes back to the house. Then he takes Brendan's car. He goes to his girlfriend's house. They go for a drive.

At the Caseys' house

1 *We understand. It's hard for Kevin. Maybe you and Kevin can come to the farm. You're our family. Come home with us.*

2 *That's very nice. Maybe we need that. But I just don't know about Kevin.*

Brendan, Anne, and Rebecca are talking about Kevin. They are worried about him. But they understand his problems.

A Breakdown

Kevin and Laura go to their special place.

1 *Kevin, I like you. But I'm seeing other guys in college.*

2 *I know. But I don't like it.*

She asks him about his future. He doesn't know. She tells him about her classes at college. He doesn't care. Laura doesn't have time for him anymore. Kevin is hurt and angry.

At the Caseys' house

Brendan can't find his car keys. He looks in the house. Rebecca and Anne also look for the keys.

They go out. Brendan's car isn't there. They go back to the house. Rebecca calls Kevin's friends. She can't find Kevin.

Kevin comes home. Rebecca, Brendan, and Anne are very angry at him. They were worried about him.

Kevin goes out. Rebecca goes after him.

In the park

Rebecca sees Kevin. He's crying. Rebecca feels sorry for him.

Kevin can talk about his father now. Rebecca feels close to him. She understands his problems. She loves her brother. They go home.

A Call for Help

At the Caseys' house

I'm sorry about the car.

Kevin, it's over. We understand.

Kevin and Rebecca go home. Brendan and Anne are
waiting. Kevin is sorry about the car.

Kevin, we can do anything. We can stay here, go to San Francisco, or go to the farm. What do you want?

I don't know. Maybe I can try the farm.

The next day, Brendan talks to Kevin about the farm. It's a
good place for Kevin and Rebecca. They can think about
their future there. Rebecca and Kevin are going to talk
about it later. Kevin's not sure.

At Sandy and Jack's house

Sandy calls Rebecca. She's leaving Jack. He hit her too many times. She asks Rebecca for help. Brendan drives Rebecca and Kevin to Sandy's house.

Jack comes into the room. Sandy is packing. Jack gets very angry.

Jack hits her.

Sandy goes to another room. She closes the door. She doesn't open the door for Jack. Jack leaves.

Kevin and Rebecca come into Sandy's house. It's a mess. Things are all over the floor.

Changes

At Sandy and Jack's house

Jack comes back. Sandy is leaving. Rebecca and Kevin are helping her. Jack gets very angry.

Sandy goes back to the house. She calls for help. Jack fights with Rebecca. Kevin fights with Jack.

The police come. They take Jack away.

The police tell Sandy about the women's shelter. Women like Sandy can go to shelters. Men like Jack can't hit them there.

At the shelter

Sandy goes to the shelter. The other women there are very nice. Sandy feels better about her life.

At the Caseys' house

Rebecca and Kevin are packing. They are going to go to the Caseys' farm in Illinois.

At a restaurant

Sandy and Rebecca are having coffee together. Sandy is going to leave the shelter in a few days.

At the Caseys' house

Kevin and Rebecca are leaving their house. They look around for the last time. They remember the sad times and the good times.

The Farm

At the Caseys' farm in Illinois

Brendan drives Kevin and Rebecca to the farm in Illinois. He shows them the red barn. The farm is big and beautiful. Then they all go into the house.

1 *Did you really make this ice cream?*

2 *Yes, I did.*

3 *It's great.*

Anne welcomes Rebecca and Kevin. She gives Kevin her special home-made ice cream.

Anne shows Rebecca her room. She shows Rebecca a picture of her son, Michael. Anne tells Rebecca about Michael's wife, Peggy, and their children, Kate and Erin. Michael and his family are coming for the Thanksgiving holiday.

Brendan shows Kevin and Rebecca the barn. He tells them about farm work.

That night, Brendan shows Kevin his computer. He uses the computer for the farm. They talk about the farm.

Kevin goes to Rebecca's room. He tells her about Brendan and the farm.

The next day, Kevin works with Brendan on the farm. He likes the farm. He's happy there.

Kevin and Brendan talk about the future. Kevin is going to stay on the farm.